The **STEP-BY-STEP** *guide to*

BUILD
YOUR
BRAND

16 STEPS FOR CREATING & MAINTAINING AN UNFORGETTABLE BUSINESS

SHERALYN PRATT

Book Design and Illustrations: Sheralyn Pratt

First Printing, 2015

ISBN 978-0-9743331-4-4

Wicked Sassy, LLC
Salt Lake City, Utah

www.wickedsassy.com

BUILD YOUR BRAND

"Make it, master it, then matter."

–Daymond John, *FUBU*

TABLE OF CONTENTS

GETTING STARTED

If you picked up this book of your own accord, chances are you fall into one of the following categories:

- You are (considering) starting up a business
- You are a creative individual looking to sell unique products (an artist, author, jewelry maker, etc.)
- You work for an established small business that is having difficulty transitioning from a startup to a mid-sized company
- You work at a large company and want to better understand the mentality behind your company's strict branding guidelines

If one of the above descriptions sounds like you, then this book is going to be very useful.

This book of branding essentials moves quickly and is action focused. Your time is valuable, and if you're self-employed you're probably already working overtime, so this book isn't looking to use any more of your time than necessary.

> **Part One** quickly explains what branding is and why it's a current necessity in business.

> **Part Two** communicates the essential steps of branding in plain English and puts you on track to immediately build your brand.

The methodology in this book is based on a quote, generally attributed to Albert Einstein or Richard Feynman, that states:

"If you can't explain it to a six year old, you don't understand it yourself."

Maybe they both said it. Who knows? Either way, this sentiment reflects the approach of this book. After reading each section, you should understand *what* needs to be done, *why* it needs to be done, and be able to immediately jump into action and strengthen your brand.

To help you move through this process, keep your eyes open for the following icons throughout this book, and let's get started!

Getting it Right: A real-world example

Brainstorm ways to apply the concept to your brand

Hint

Game

PART
ONE

WHAT IS A BRAND?

A brand is a combination of many aspects of a business. Just like you are more than a pretty face, the branding for your venture is more than just a logo. Your brand is what you do, how you do it, and how you and your product fit into the world.

Put simply: Your brand is the strategic packaging of your reputation.

A **strong** brand creates:

- High name recognition
- Awareness of product offerings and differentiators
- A reputable service/product with a vision
- Strong messaging
- Relevance in the world at large

A **weak** brand has:

- No story or vision
- Low and/or no understanding of product differentiators
- Unknown and/or unclear values and mission
- Standards that gauge success solely on the amount of money it takes in
- No role in the world at large

WHY BRANDING IS NO LONGER OPTIONAL

For several years now "branding" has been a buzz word in nearly every industry. Why? Because your brand creates a reputation that lets customers know how much they can trust you to deliver on your promise.

A helpful way to think about brand is to say that your brand is what people say about your product or service when you're not in the room.

- Have people even heard of your brand?
- Are people familiar with messaging or values that allows them to concisely and accurately describe your brand in one sentence?
- Do people know what makes you

different and why your differentiator is important to a buying decision?

In the pre-internet world, branding was typically a game big boys played. If you were small and local, you didn't need to brand yourself. Word of mouth did that for you. A small local business could hang out a shingle, package all its products in a generic bag, and still have customers know where and how to find them because everyone knew every business in town.

Things have changed in the 21st century. We now have an entire rising generation who has never lived without the internet. This emerging market often deems brick-and-mortar shopping as option-limiting and time-expensive. With the internet, we're seeing huge changes in how products are brought to market and how services are delivered.

For example, before the days of the internet, most businesses didn't ship purchases to customers. If you wanted Ghirardelli chocolate, then you literally had to go to San Francisco. Up until just a few decades ago, small businesses and local specialists took care of the niche needs of local markets with little fanfare or competition.

Those days are officially gone.

Small businesses not only compete with the big boys now, but a small local business also competes with similar small businesses in other cities. Unless you provide a hands-on service like massage, your next door neighbor may end up buying a product you sell from a competitor 1,000 miles away. And they'll base that purchasing decision on price, perceived quality, and whether or not they think the online brand is reputable.

THE CURRENT MARKET

In the current online market, the importance of reputation cannot be overstated.

Let's say you're in the market to buy a protective case for your new cell phone. You go to your local mall to check out cases and see that the cases you like are between $40-60. Curious if that's the best price, you pull out your phone while you're still in the store and look up the same phone cases on Amazon. Your search shows that Amazon has more colors available of the cases you like with prices between $20-25.

More options at half the price? You politely leave the store and finish your shopping online.

As you dig into Amazon's phone case offerings, you notice that the case you liked most at the mall has an average rating of 3.1 out of 5 stars based on 2,132 reviews. Curious as to why it's not rated higher, you click on the reviews and start seeing headlines like: *Looks Good But Didn't Save My Phone* and *Don't Expect a Miracle*.

As you read about the experiences others have had with your current favorite phone case, you see a trend emerge. Like you, others were attracted to the case for its sleek look, but were disappointed that it didn't protect their phone as they'd hoped.

How likely are you to buy this case?

You do some more browsing and find another case you like. Its product description claims it's the best, but there are only five reviews and they all sound like they came from employees, not actual customers.

How likely are you to buy this second case?

You keep looking and see a third case. This same case had been at the store in the mall as well, but it's not your favorite-looking option. Yet, when you look at the reviews, you see this case has an average rating of 4.7 out of 5 stars with 5,817 reviews. When you check out what other customers are saying about the case, you end up reading tale after tale of people who thought they'd destroyed their phone only to find it in pristine condition, thanks to the case.

How likely are you to buy this third case?

If form is more important to you than function, you may buy case #1. If you're a habitual risk taker who likes to be in on new things, you may choose case #2. But if you are in the market for a case to protect an expensive investment from harm, buying case #3—or a case made by the same company—for $20 becomes a no brainer. With over 5,000 people giving it a thumbs up, you now trust it to be a wise investment.

And where there is a clear customer understanding that a company or individual will consistently deliver as promised, a brand (i.e., reputation) is born.

IT'S ALL ABOUT TRUST

Amazon knows the importance of product and seller trustworthiness, as does every other online retailer. Increasingly, websites that facilitate third-party sales are requiring customers to leave reviews of their experience so the host can weed out weak sellers and fraudulent accounts.

If you're eBay and you have a bunch of fake sellers ripping people off, your eBay brand will depreciate quickly. For this reason, companies like eBay must make huge efforts to identify and disassociate from sellers who don't support their standards for quality. Repairing trust after it has been violated is an uphill battle that is very easily lost. To avoid this as much as possible, sites like eBay, Etsy, and Amazon use customer reviews to turn their sellers into mini-brands that support their larger brand.

Reviews: A Snapshot of Your Brand

Reviews breed trust online. Just like in the phone case example above, the more reviews you have with a common narrative, the greater the sense of perceived trust. This is why an online seller with no customer feedback is approached with more caution than a seller who has been delivering as promised for seven years. No one coaches prospective customers to trust one seller over the other. Customers do this instinctively.

If your brand has no documented track history and the competition has a strong reputation, then you have some catching up to do. Even if you offer identical items at the same price, most people will choose to buy from the reputable brand. And if you drop your price 10% or even 20%, customers will still likely go with the reputable seller—assuming your product is lower quality. Why else would your item be so cheap?

Value and Brand Go Hand-in-Hand

Many marketers will tell you that brands that create a strong value proposition don't have to worry about competing with their prices, and this is largely true. Every day consumers buy a brand name item for more money when a generically packaged version of the same product sits next to it for a fraction of the price. The two items are literally made in the same factory with the same equipment by the same people, but one has a label that is trusted more so it gets the sale.

This is the power of branding.

Whether you're a business owner selling widgets, a local coffee shop selling premium brews, or a creative person trying to become a power player in your industry, your branding matters.

If your branding is weak, you will be perceived as less-than even if you are technically the best. If you are unable or unwilling to effectively communicate your brand value to the marketplace, you will struggle on an otherwise thriving vine.

So consider the sixteen branding elements outlined in Part Two of this book as sixteen would-be employees who are willing to work for free. You can:

a. Put them to work by clarifying what each branding element should say when you're not in the room

b. Leave your branding elements unemployed by giving them nothing to do

c. Let your competition create messaging that puts your branding elements to work for them

Completing your branding pyramid and implementing it every day is like hiring sixteen free employees who appear anywhere in the world and advocate for you whenever you are mentioned. And what business doesn't need that?

FORBES TOP 10

Forbes magazine put out its 2014 list of the world's Top 100 Most Valuable Brands.

- What do you think the chances are that

you have heard of all 100 companies?

- What are the chances you recognize their logos?
- What are the chances you know their taglines?
- What are the chances that if you easily match their logo with their tagline that you have also purchased something from them?

Let's see how well the Top 10 companies are doing at creating messaging that sticks. Can you correctly match the tagline and logo of each company?

1. 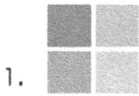 2. Google 3.

4. SAMSUNG 5.  6. IBM

7.  8. Coca-Cola 9. LV
LOUIS VUITTON

A.) *Think different.*

B.) *Let's go places.*   10.

C.) *Don't be evil.*

D.) *Building a smarter planet.*

E.) *Imagine.*

F.) *Empowering us all.*

G.) *Open happiness.*

H.) *Epileather.*

I.) *Imagination at work.*

J.) *I'm lovin' it.*

Did you get 100%?

(1=F, 2=C, 3=A, 4=E, 5=B, 6=D, 7=J, 8=G, 9=H, 10=I)

I can promise you that each of these companies hope that you did, since each company individually spends millions every year to ensure that you have instant recall of their existence.

As much as these companies seem like behemoths today, they didn't start out that way. Like any company, they started small and had their fair share of growing pains. In the beginning, they were a simple seed of an idea that sprouted into a fledgling business and grew from there. How they dealt with both their challenges and successes gradually built the brands, reputations, and products you recognize today.

BUILDING BRAND POWER

The makers of Pepsi have always been of the opinion that Pepsi tastes better than Coca-Cola. Back in 1975, they decided to put their money where their mouth was and hold the Pepsi Challenge. They put Pepsi and Coke in plain cups, asked shoppers to take a sip of each, then asked them to choose the best-tasting cola.

The results were exactly what Pepsi wanted them to be: Pepsi won!

So the good news for Pepsi? Over 50% of blind taste testers preferred the *taste* of Pepsi.

The bad news for Pepsi? Over 50% of shoppers who were not blindfolded still preferred to *buy* Coke.

Why?

Pepsi has repeated this same "we taste better!" campaign several times since 1975 with largely the same results. In fact, a recent taste test showed that 50% of participants preferred the taste of Pepsi to Coke, and yet 75% of the same participants said they would still buy Coke before Pepsi.

So when 25% of the people buying Coke prefer the taste of Pepsi, what are they buying when they choose Coca-Cola?

Are they buying function? Values? Style? Image? A feeling? An identity? All of the above?

If you said all of the above (and then some), you are on the right track. Because as much as people will tell you that a brand is nothing more than your logo, a brand is decidedly more than that. Brand loyalty can result in the exact phenomenon that has baffled Pepsi executives for decades: Customers can try a competing product, admit it's better, but then *still* walk away loyal to the brand they've just claimed is second best.

One reason for this is that the sixteen free employees in your brand pyramid do a lot of work. They connect people to:

- The foundation and benefits of your brand
- Your brand emotions and personality
- Your branded style and image
- A face they know and can trust

As Coke has learned, defining and maintaining these identifiers will help you create a brand identity that retains customers even in the face of a taste test that doesn't swing your way. Coke will stay away from the taste tests. Those clearly aren't Coke's thing. But that's okay! Over time, Coca-Cola has found what works for them, and they're sticking with it.

So should you.

SIMPLE ≠ UNESSENTIAL

If you own a business, you know that the little things add up. Money adds up. Actions add up. Attitudes definitely add up.

How many simple things do you or your employees do every day that have far-reaching consequences?

Turning on an oven is simple, but if a baker doesn't turn the oven on every day there will be no baked goods to sell. Wiping water spots off of silverware at a 5-star restaurant may be simple, but if workers start putting out spotted silverware day-after-day, how long will the restaurant keep its 5-star rating?

Sometimes we spend so much time aiming high that we become blind to the stepping stones beneath our feet that take us to that higher ground. This is what brand is all about: a platform obsessed with the basic stepping stones.

When viewed holistically from afar the pieces disappear into a whole. The larger and stronger the company, the smaller the seams between each branding building block appear. And when the company gets big enough, strong branding appears to be unassailable, seamless, and "too big to fail."

SIMPLE STEPS, STACKED HIGH

The brand pyramid you are about to complete has universal application across industries. It doesn't matter if you work with services or products, this pyramid applies to you and is a firm foundation for building your brand. The four tiers of your branding pyramid will explore the function and purpose of your business, your values and personality, your visual style, and your logo.

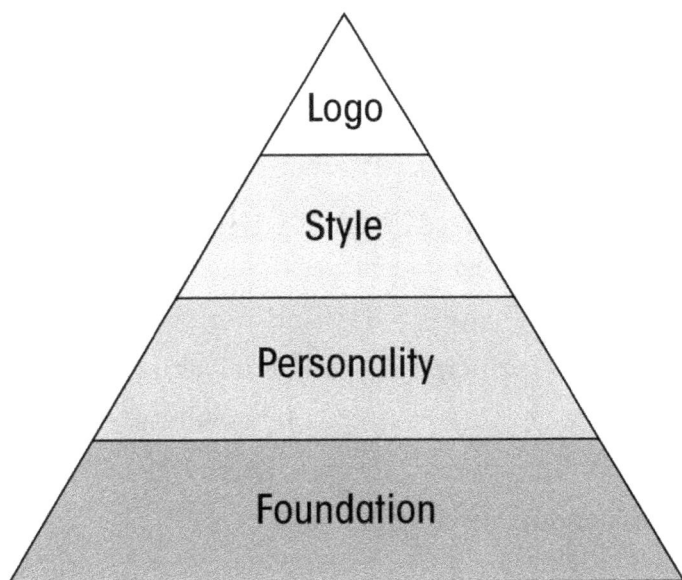

Some people believe that just the top tier— your logo—is your brand. That's because jargon can easily be confused.

When a rancher brands cattle, for example, their "brand" is literally the mark burned into the animal. So, yes, a physical mark can be a brand, but if you're branding correctly then that mark means something. Do you think, even centuries ago, that thieves regarded each branded steer equally? Do you think some brands were known for being higher-quality livestock, or that some of the ranchers had reputation of seeking out stolen livestock and getting even?

Even centuries ago, a brand on livestock was not simply a mark. The mark was a signifier of what you were getting (or getting into) when interacting with that brand.

The same story today and hinges on many of the same principles. And it all starts with the function and purpose of your business.

Within these four tiers are sixteen components of your brand.

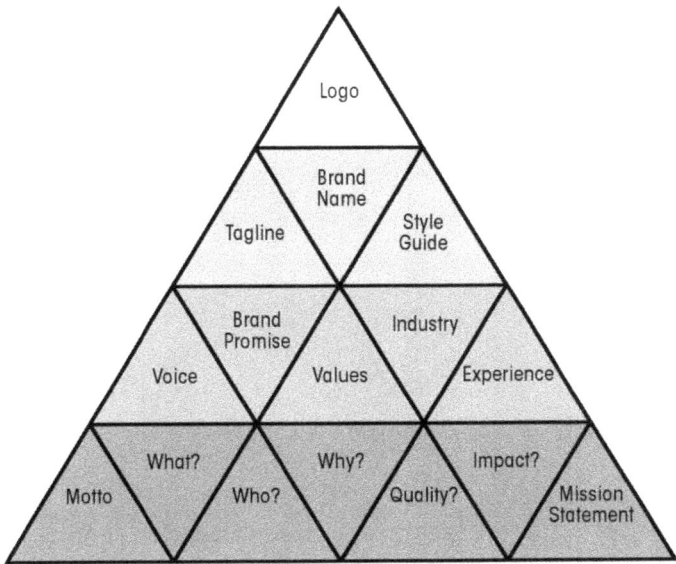

Each of these blocks play a role in communicating what you do, why you do it, and the value you bring to the marketplace.

PART
TWO

START BUILDING YOUR FOUNDATION

Your brand's foundation is comprised of:

- Your motto (cornerstone)
- Your answers to 5 questions
- Your mission statement (cornerstone)

It's not an overestimation to say that 95% of companies skip defining a solid foundation before launching their business. In their defense, they don't skip laying their foundation because they are lazy; they skip it because everything seems so clear in their minds that it almost seems silly to write it all out. It's only when they realize that customers aren't aware of basic information that they realize they've left seven "free employees" with nothing to do or say, at which point they start clarifying foundations retroactively.

> ❗ Never assume customers know *why* you're in business and why they should choose you.

The foundation of your custom branding pyramid brings everyone up to speed on what you do, why you do it, and how you do it better. Helping customers understand these elements of your business involves thoughtfully implementing seven assets—two cornerstones and the answers to five clarifying questions.

Let's start with the five questions that will help you define and support your cornerstones.

5 Questions

The foundation of your brand can be identified by answering the five questions support and connect the cornerstones in the foundation tier of your brand pyramid.

Question 1: What do you sell?

Question 2: Who is your target audience?

Question 3: Why should consumers buy your

product/service? (What is the difference between you and competitors?)

Question 4: What do you stand for?

Question 5: How does your company impact the world at large?

BRAINSTORM TIME

Take a few minutes to answer each of the five questions in writing. And don't worry, you can always come back and change answers. Just get something down right now, because this is your foundation. Everything else you will add in future tiers builds on these answers.

If you feel stuck or uninspired on any of the questions, check out the tips and quick examples for each question below to get things rolling.

Tips on Question 1—What do you sell?

Your initial answers to this question may be a one-word response like:

- Cars
- Coffee
- Massages

- Widgets

But once you have the noun of what you sell, don't be afraid to add an adjective into there. Maybe you sell:

- *Sexy* cars
- *Savory* coffee
- *Healing* massages
- *Nerdy* widgets

Don't get too narrow in your description here—leave yourself room to grow—but don't be afraid to throw an adjective or two into your response either. Then use the adjectives you've chosen to see what truly binds you and your customers together.

Why?

Chances are that your loyal customers value the adjectives you offer (i.e., sexy, savory, healing, nerdy) at least as much as they value the nouns (i.e., cars, coffee, massages, widgets).

Last of all, once you have the right combination of adjectives and nouns, take a closer look at the values your descriptions support to define what you're *really* selling:

- Sex appeal
- Indulgent empowerment
- Health and comfort
- Identity with a tribe

TRADER JOE'S

Trader Joe's is a health-conscious grocery store with an arguably cult-like following of people who like high-quality products at affordable prices. At Trader Joe's, gorgeous flower arrangements for under $10 make every day the perfect day to give someone a bouquet. Affordable wine means you never have to show up to a party empty-handed. And the high-quality food products Trader Joe's carries are pretty much exclusive to them. You can't go buy a Trader Joe's item somewhere else. . . but you can go down the road to another health food store and pay more for a similar item.

If you declare that you hate Trader Joe's at a party, people may look at you like you just kicked a kitten. Why? Because Trader Joe's in-house brand is solid, and if you go to their website, they'll spell out what they sell (and how they stand behind it) as follows:

Trader Joe's private label products promise great quality fare for exceptional, everyday prices. We taste everything before we put our name on it and offer only what we feel is extraordinary. We tried it. We like it. If you don't, bring it back for a refund or exchange — no hassles.

When you see our name on a label, you can be assured that the product contains:

- *NO artificial flavors or preservatives*
- *NO synthetic colors*
- *NO MSG*
- *NO genetically modified ingredients*
- *NO partially hydrogenated oils (artificial trans-fats)*
- *NO "marketing" costs*
- *YES tasting panel approval*
- *YES quality ingredients*
- *YES great price*

(Content from www.traderjoes.com)

Trader Joe's food sales are a byproduct of what they are really selling: Values.

Trader Joe's is selling quality. They're selling natural flavor. They're selling trust. This is a platform that allows them to control current inventory while also creating an inherent screening process for new and exciting products that will be a match for their current customer as they move into the future.

If a new product meets all of the listed

requirements, it can be added into inventory. If not, it belongs in a different store with different values. No product is worth breaking a customer's trust, and Trader Joe's knows it.

When considering Question 1, think about what are you really selling and how can you define it in a way that helps you to continue to introduce new products and services without alienating your target customer.

⚡ WHAT (NOUNS) DO YOU SELL?

What?

WHAT (ADJECTIVES) DO YOU SELL?

What?

WHAT (VALUES) DO YOU SELL?

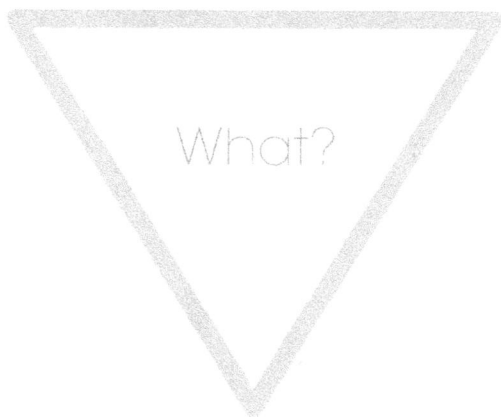

What?

WHAT (BENEFITS) DO YOU SELL?

What?

Tips on Question 2—Who is your target audience?

I have never spoken with a start-up business owner who has a strategic answer to this question. Not once. Why do I say that? Because most small businesses aim too broadly when targeting their ideal customer.

For example:

- If they're a plumber, they think their customer is *anyone* with a toilet.
- If an author has written a book, they think it's a book *anyone* could enjoy.
- If an artist designs shirts, they think their market is *anyone* with a chest and torso.
- If a business is making steering wheel covers, they think their market is *anyone* who owns a car.

No, no, no, and no. Even Walmart can't target customers with such broad strokes. In fact, most companies benefit more from approaching from the opposite extreme and targeting a very narrow market.

👍 APPLE

If you remember, the #1 company on Forbes 2014 list of most valuable brands was Apple, and they are a fascinating case study in identifying one's target customer.

Now, if you are an Apple-phile, please don't be offended when I point out that Apple has not always been #1 in the computer world. Apple has definitely had its fair share growing pains when it comes to gaining market share. Back in the twentieth century, Apple's high price tag and incompatible software allowed competitors like IBM, Hewlett-Packard, Microsoft, and many others to successfully edge Apple out of the work place.

Yet, ultimately, it wasn't usurping Microsoft's hold on the workplace as the word processor of choice that took Apple to #1. The shift in power occurred when Apple embraced the fact that all work and no play made Mac a dull boy. Forget boring documents! Apple needed to position Macs as the go-to technology for people who were all about art and expression and music. And given how rampant digital piracy was in the early 2000s, Apple knew exactly what people wanted: they wanted what came to be known as iTunes—the ability to buy portable music at an easy-to-stomach price.

After decades of trying to get a solid foothold in the market, Apple had finally found its sweet spot in addressing the digital piracy epidemic. The day Apple made it their goal to get all their customers to legally buy all their music through iTunes was the day Apple started marching up the path to #1.

Training consumers to buy music files that were only playable on Apple software put the entire music industry on the path of going digital. This same digital revolution then expanded to include movies and other forms of entertainment (and is now copied by other companies wanting a piece of the digital pie).

How serious is Apple about having you buy every form of entertainment through their iStore? Well, they've started removing CD/DVD drives from their latest hardware offerings. No more uploading CDs or DVDs to your computer. If you want content on your iPhone, iPod, iPad, or any other iDevice, you need to buy it through

Apple.

And this dynamic came to pass all because Apple made the choice to say: Our target customer wants access to their music at all times. Let's do that.

And they did.

As you consider how Question 2 applies to your brand, remember that the answer may not be what you think it is. Use any validated research or hard data you have at your disposal as your guide and ask yourself: Who am I helping, and how?

WHO IS YOUR TARGET AUDIENCE?

Who?

Tips on Question 3—Why buy you? (What is the difference between you and competitors?)

This question is a biggie. A customer usually has several competitors to choose from—some of which are very likely cheaper. So why should this customer choose you?

What will a customer get from you that they won't get from the competition?

Maybe your differentiator is that you *are* the cheapest. No one undersells you and that's a promise! But only one business in each industry gets to legitimately make that claim, so chances are you have a unique differentiator that propelled you into your industry.

What is it?

- Affordability
- Improved quality
- Shared values
- Increased capabilities
- New benefits
- Filling a current market gap

Your answer to Question 3 can address both what you do and how you do it—or what your customer does and how they do it. It can also include awards you or users earn or differences that make you stand apart from the competition.

👍 SHANE CO.

Shane Co. is a national jewelry chain. It's by no means the largest jeweler in America, but its brand keeps growing because it knows its differentiators.

- Your friend, Tom Shane, has spent decades developing strong business relationships that get you the best product for the best deal.
- Shane Co. cuts out the middle man, handpicking their jewels one at a time before leaving their castoffs to be bought by other jewelers.
- Exclusive designs mean you won't see your jewelry on someone else.

Another differentiator is Shane Co.'s consistent use of the owner's voice in all of their radio advertisements. While other brands switch out voice-over talents and actors from commercial to commercial, Shane Co. sticks with the same dry, nasal tones of owner, Tom Shane. And in a sea of radio songs and commercials that are trying to sound perfect, Tom Shane sounds homespun and under-produced, and that's a differentiator.

If you don't know Shane Co. is a thriving national chain and you hear their commercials, the Shane Co. commercials might get you to believe that Shane Co. is a little-guy upstart that's trying to get your local business away from the jeweler giants.

Why? Because of their message reassuring you that Shane Co. is:

- "Your friend in the diamond business"
- Hands-on in selecting only the finest jewels for you to choose from
- Friends with sellers who always let them buy diamonds their competitors never even got to see
- Committed to creating one-of-a-kind designs you won't see anywhere else

So when answering why people should buy your brand over the competition, think about not only what you do, but *how* you do it. Then think about how that can be a value-add to your customers. Write down everything you can think of and then simplify them into bullets. And remember, your answers should be simple, straightforward, and easy to understand.

WHY BUY YOU (DIFFERENTIATORS)?

Why?

Tips on Question 4—What do you stand for?

There is no universal right or wrong answer to this question. The answer will be your truth and because the value is such a deep part of you, it will somehow be embedded in your product.

Maybe you're a magician invested in filling the world with childlike wonder, or a comedian who uses humor to keep people aware of current events in the world. Maybe you're a mechanic who never overcharges a naïve customer, or an Amish man who builds luxury campers without using electricity or modern tools in your process.

Each of these individuals have their product, but they also have the following values built-in to their products:

> **Magician:** Keeping wonder alive
>
> **Comedian:** Laughing at the status quo when it deserves it
>
> **Mechanic:** Being honest when others might not be
>
> **Amish man:** Continuing traditional, handcrafted excellence

Your answer to this question will not

necessarily be business related. Your answer should stem from the personal ethics that drive you on a day-to-day basis.

Another way to ask yourself this question is to say: If my product or service made me overwhelmingly rich, what would there be more of in the world? Or, what causes would I donate to or what issues would I fix?

The answers to these questions matter can be built into your business and communicated to customers in a way that will help you stand apart from the competition.

CHIPOTLE

The last century has shown a massive shift in how and what people eat in developed countries. Farming and ranching have been drastically altered to meet the demands of an ever-growing market. For example, a few years back it was reported that a half a billion chickens were required to provide Buffalo wings on Super Bowl Sunday *alone*.

In a financially driven market aimed at providing more and more meat for less and less money, animals universally come out as the losers. Chipotle knows this and they've taken a stand.

If you have never eaten at Chipotle, it is a franchised Mexican grill specializing in burritos and tacos. Its menu requires a lot of meat, but the company has chosen to be very specific in its meat requirements. They believe in animal rights, so if you wish to sell your meat to Chipotle, they are going to come tour your facilities.

What will they be looking for?

It's important to Chipotle that animals they source have lived natural lives. So if your pigs spend their lives in a pen, Chipotle is not interested in your meat. If your cattle aren't free-range, then Chipotle will pass. If your dairy cows don't have daily access to outdoor pastures, the Chipotle representative may just chastise you before s/he leaves. And if you pump your chickens full of antibiotics or hormones, Chipotle won't touch them.

Chipotle is in the meat business, but Chipotle loyalists will be quick to inform you of how all the ingredients are ethically sourced. Yes, they may be eating beef, but it's from an animal that lived a good, natural life.

This matters to Chipotle ownership just as much as it matters to all the loyal customers that could easily go eat somewhere else, but don't.

So as you consider Question 4, take a look at how your personal ethics inform the product or service you are providing. Think about the words and causes others use when describing you. What do you value, and how has that value made its way into your business?

Chipotle builds company policy about ethical treatment of animals, while the ownership of Chick-fil-A feels so strongly about their Christian faith that they are closed on Sundays. These policies are values that may cause you to connect or disconnect with these companies as a customer, and Chipotle and Chick-fil-A fully accept the consequences of allowing these values to be brand identifiers.

Is Chick-fil-A a more controversial company than Chipotle? I think most people would agree that it is. The values inserted into their brand are arguably more divisive than the values of a cigarette company like Marlboro. I point this out not to tell you that you *should* be controversial, but to clarify that there is room for everyone in business and if you have values, there is no reason to hide them.

Maybe you believe in obsessive cleanliness.

Maybe you believe in volunteering time in the community.

Maybe you love animals and support a local rescue or shelter.

Maybe you believe in daily exercise.

Maybe you keep your eye on the latest fashion.

There is a nearly endless list of qualities and values that can help you attract customers who want what you are offering, so if you don't think you have a value-based brand identifier, think again. We all do. And if you still come up empty, then ask around, take a look at what you've "liked" recently on social media, or take a personality quiz to get your wheels turning on where your values lie and how they inform your work.

There is no right answer for Question 4. There is only an authentic answer.

WHAT DO YOU STAND FOR?

Quality

Tips on Question 5— How do you impact the world at large?

This question seems similar to Question 3, but this is really more of a combination of Questions 1 thru 4. Think of the question more in these terms:

If you were to become the goliath of your industry—like Apple—how would the industry change? How would your audience change? How would the world change?

The answer to this question can be large or small, but your answer should pass the six-year-old test and be a statement a child can comprehend.

Maybe if you rise to the top of your industry no one would ever eat corn syrup again, or maybe prescription glasses would never again be a source of pressure-point headaches. Maybe all software would become freeware, or maybe every home would have recycling services.

Your vision may be small or large. Scope doesn't matter. What matters is that you can see it and explain it in one sentence that is easy for anyone else to understand.

MCDONALD'S

McDonald's is an example of a business leader literally changing the world. Founder Ray Kroc brought the assembly line into fast food and automated the food-making process. Despite the fact that few people openly champion McDonald's for having the best food, they still serve over 70 million customers each day.

Why?

The ease, accessibility, predictability, and uniformity of McDonald's menu offerings clearly holds an appeal. That appeal has empowered ethics that have shaped the food industry as a whole. And that industry is literally shaping the human race—how we eat, what we eat, and the (im)balance of our calorie intake.

The automation of food, making formerly scarce and laborious-to-prepare meats easily accessible, may have literally changed how humans eat for the rest of time. In this regard, Ray Kroc changed the world. That is his legacy, and he's proud of it.

If you were an industry leader, how would your business practices change the industry and maybe even world? How would you change the world, and what legacy would you be proud of?

HOW DO YOU IMPACT THE WORLD?

Impact

YOUR BRAND CORNERSTONES: MOTTO AND MISSION STATEMENT

Now that you have completed five of the seven foundation stones, it's time to use the material your brainstormed with each question to help you form your brand cornerstones.

- Your brand motto
- Your brand mission statement

As you build your pyramid, these cornerstones will likely go through multiple revisions before being finalized. Right now you're in brainstorm mode, so don't worry about getting your motto or mission statement perfect on the first take. Feel free to be scattered and wordy as you brainstorm. It's okay. Get anything down that comes to mind then come back to it later and refine. It's all part of the process.

Then, once you have your motto and mission statement nailed down, carve them in stone.

Brand Motto

Your brand motto is something you or your

employees can say as a mantra as you work to encourage optimal products or customer service. This is separate from your tagline.

HOW ARE TAGLINES AND MOTTOS DIFFERENT?

We will discuss taglines later. A **tagline** is phrase used to help customers identify you in the marketplace. Taglines embody the marketing message of a company, and are used in advertisements.

Examples include:

- JUST DO IT
- I'm lovin' it!
- Can you hear me now?
- Be a hero

You, as a customer, likely recognize most of these taglines (Nike, McDonalds, Verizon, GoPro), but these are separate from internal company mottos.

Nike doesn't want all their employees to "just do it"… whatever *it* might be, and an employee who's "lovin' it" isn't necessarily providing great customer service.

In short, remember:

- Taglines are for customers
- Mottos are for employees

For the moment, we'll focus only on your motto.

Creating a Motto that Works

Your brand motto should inform quality parameters for employees across all job descriptions. It can be helpful to think of it as a memorable mantra brand insiders can recite to remind them how to deliver on brand promises. This mantra is your company motto and Guy Kawasaki advises that you make yours "short, sweet, and swallowable."

Unlike the marketing taglines, you are very unlikely to recognize a company motto unless you have worked within its walls. Examples include:

- Customer service so good people tell stories about it.
- Make something you love.
- Style to the people.
- Get it first, get it right.

You don't know what companies these mottos belong to, and that's okay. Their employees do, which is important because these are internal calls to action.

You would never want your marketing tagline to be "Customer service so good people tell stories about it," and yet an employee in an unusual customer service situation can use the phrase as a lighthouse to guide them to a good solution.

Same goes with "Make something you love." If the company culture is make sure that employees are consistently developing things they want and love, then making their mantra match that call to action makes sense and will actively weed out ideas that are less than inspiring.

CREATE YOUR FIRST CORNERSTONE

Now that you know who your motto speaks to (you and your employees), it's time to brainstorm mottos that are a match for your business.

What is a mantra you can all say as you work?

What is a motto you want everyone to live up to?

Keep it simple. Keep it straightforward. Great companies are built on simple mottos everyone remembers.

⚡ MOTTO BRAINSTORM

Motto

Your Mission Statement

The term *mission statement* sounds intense and serious, but it doesn't have to be. At its heart, a mission statement is simply what you do, why you do it, and who you do it for. It can be simple; it can be elaborate. It's all up to you.

The purpose of a mission statement is to let the world know what to expect from you—no flowery words or legalese required. Be succinct and feel free to see if it passes the six-year-old comprehension test.

The perfect place to see the role of mission statements in business in the TV show *The Shark Tank*. In this unique approach to reality TV, real-life millionaire and billionaire investors invite small business owners to come pitch their business or product. There is no narrow niche the companies must fit into to pitch to the Shark investors, but to gain an investment from one of the Sharks, a business owner must convince these savvy business people that they are a wise investment.

In each episode, every hopeful candidate answers the same questions for the Sharks.

- Who's your market and how do you help them?
- Why does the market need you, specifically?
- How does everyone benefit when you succeed?

The good news is that you've already answered five questions in the previous section that spell all this out.

Question 1: What do you sell?

Question 2: Who is your target audience?

Question 3: Why should consumers buy your product/service? (What is the difference between you and competitors?)

Question 4: What do you stand for?

Question 5: How does your company impact the world at large?

As you move forward through this book, you'll see that the answers to all of these questions come into play again and again. So if you skimmed over answering these questions, backtrack and thoughtfully answer each question before coming back to get started on your mission statement.

REAL-WORLD MISSION STATEMENTS

Take a look at some mission statement examples from successful companies.

Trader Joe's

"The mission of Trader Joe's is to give our customers the best food and beverage values that they can find anywhere and to provide them with the information required to make informed buying decisions. We provide these with a dedication to the highest quality of customer satisfaction delivered with a sense of warmth, friendliness, fun, individual pride, and company spirit."

IKEA

"At IKEA our goal is to create a better everyday life for the many people. Our business idea supports this vision by offering a wide range of well-designed, functional home furnishing products at prices so low that as many people as possible will be able to afford them."

Patagonia

"Build the best product, cause no unnecessary harm, use business to inspire and implement solutions to the environmental crisis."

CREATE YOUR SECOND CORNERSTONE

Be thoughtful when crafting your mission statement, but not pretentious. There is no need to present yourself as anything you're not. The more honest you are, the simpler the statement will be. And the simpler it is, the more it will resonate and be remembered. That's what you're looking for.

MISSION STATEMENT BRAINSTORM

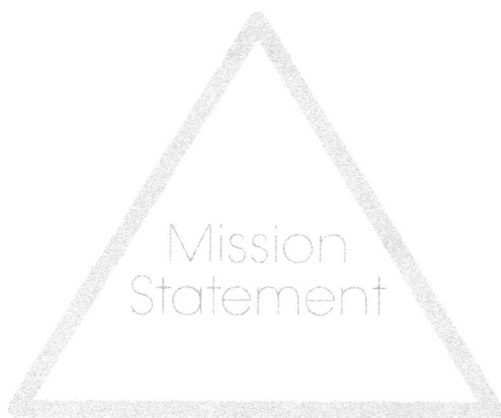

Mission Statement

FOUNDATION CONCLUSION

As you lay the foundation of your brand, take the time to write out some basic language for every building block in the foundation of your branding pyramid. There's no need to be perfect on your first draft. You will have plenty of opportunities to refine and edit, but writing things out will give you a foundation to reference as you move forward to the remaining three tiers.

Before you move on, be sure to have placeholder answers for each of the following questions:

1. What do you sell?
2. Who is your target audience?
3. Why should consumers buy your product/service? (What is the difference between you and competitors?)
4. What do you stand for?
5. How does your company impact the world at large?
6. What is your company motto?
7. What is your company mission statement?

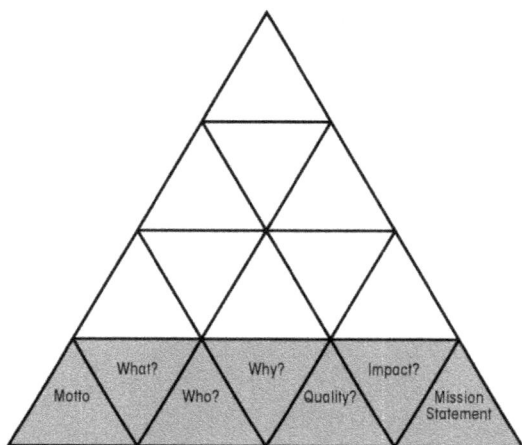

The answers to these questions are the foundation of your brand. Everything else builds on top of it. So once you have completed your foundation, you will be ready to move into Tier 2: Your Brand Personality.

YOUR BRAND PERSONALITY

The second tier of your pyramid focuses on how your brand stands apart in your industry. Your brand is more than a static entity. It should have a personality that embodies values and experiences your customers can connect with.

If your business took the Myers-Briggs test, The Color Code, or any other personality quiz, what would be the results?

You can take personality quizzes while keeping your business in mind:
- Myers-Briggs
- Color Code

Use results to help find qualities or attributes that will help connect you to your customer.

Are you fun-loving and people-pleasing, or are you rigid and quality-focused? Do you work first and play later, or do you shut your doors in perfect weather conditions and allow employees to go out and play?

There is room for every type of business, and the more clearly you communicate your values the more likely you are to connect with customers who share your values.

👍 ZAPPOS

Zappos is an online shoe retailer with a call center that is a legend in its own time. Zappos employees aren't trained to put the smallest band-aid possible on a problem. They are trained to surpass your expectations to such a degree that you might just think they're joking when they offer you free overnight delivery of shoes you forgot to pack for a wedding the next day.

Companies in this day and age don't do things like that...right?

Most don't, but Zappos does.

When you visit Zappos website, they state

that they are a company that is all about expression and that "At Zappos, We're Always Creating Fun and a Little Weirdness!" They want to help you WOW the world by first WOWing you. If that means letting you buy six pairs of shoes and return five pairs for free just to find the right style and size, well, be ready to be WOWed by their customer service. And if it means sending you flowers because the customer service representative picked up on the fact that you are having a bad day? WOW customer service allows for that.

Now ask yourself:

- How many customers do you think Zappos retains as it embraces WOWing customers with creative fun and weirdness?
- Do you think they are attracting and retaining their target customer through these policies?

Zappos may not be the right fit for every person who wears shoes, but based on their sales and customer retention, there is evidence showing a strong customer base embraces Zappos fun and permissive approach to online shoe shopping.

Competitors that support different values will catch the eye of a different customer who is looking for a little less fun and a little more of something else. For example, competitors may attract customers who are more focused on:

- Flash or overstock sales
- Confirming social status
- Pairing shoes with accessories
- Trendspotting

In each instance, choosing a brand personality helps target customers instantly connect your offerings.

As you build the second tier of your brand, keep in mind that your brand personality often has more impact on loyalty than your logo or your marketing. By embracing a personality and lifestyle you validate everyone who shares or embraces your attributes. And if some people hate your business personality? That's okay. I dare say that sometimes that's even good.

Anything that is distinct in any way is loved or hated by someone, so stop worrying about pleasing everyone. If you're so "meh" that no one objects to you, chances are that you're so bland no one remembers you either.

Stick with being memorable by choosing to create a recognizable business personality. And to have a personality you need to have a voice.

Finding Your Voice

All strong brands have a voice that expresses their personality. This voice is the tone of your messaging. Every word that is uttered or written in proximity of your brand name or logo will be associated with your brand. This means you need to clearly define this voice and keep it consistent.

DEPENDS AND HUGGIES

Respecting the fine line between diapers for babies and bladder control for adults is a minefield where even the most silver-tongued and circumspect marketing executives can unwittingly trip into dangerous territory. After all, everyone expects a baby not to have control of its bowels. Seeing a baby in diapers is par for the course. They don't know any better and they can't help it. Society accepts that and for the most part has no problem swapping horror stories in mixed company.

But once we are "potty trained," maintaining control of our bowels becomes a matter of dignity. Where and how we do the daily activity of processing food becomes highly regulated.

As a children's book so succinctly states it, "Everyone Poops," but when you're in the market of advertising to different adult demographics who may or may not make it to the bathroom on time, the voice you use to let your customer know you have what they need becomes paramount.

Below are two statements taken from ads. One of these statements is advertising Depends (adult underwear protection) and one is for Huggies (diapers for babies). One advertisement is aimed at a mother buying for a baby, and the other is aimed at a woman buying for herself.

Which ad copy do you think goes with each item?

Option 1: *New comfy fit that lasts.*

Option 2: *Confidence is always in fashion.*

As you've likely deduced, Huggies is

represented in Option #1. A "comfy fit that lasts" is exactly what a mother is looking for in a diaper. Depends uses more formal language in Option #2 to address the values of a more mature audience.

Even though Depends and Huggies are fundamentally similar products, they target different audiences. Because they target different audiences, they need to use different voices. Huggies uses words a mother might use in front of children, like comfy. Depends stays away from slang, humor, and anything undignified that makes light of their product's function.

Finding the right voice is all about knowing who you are speaking to and the words and tone they connect with.

To help keep brand voice consistent, it is common for companies to choose three adjectives that describe their voice.

GE AND MINI

GE (General Electric) and Mini Cooper are both well-known international companies. GE makes pretty much everything the modern world runs on and Mini Cooper makes sporty, compact cars.

If you think maintaining brand identity and voice is difficult as a startup business, imagine managing tens of thousands of employees around the world who speak different languages. Imagine seeing your ads translated into different languages and having to trust that the translation is true to the original concept.

Big companies like GE and Mini Cooper have to do things like this every day. They're releasing the same product in France and Japan and targeting the same customer, so the voice has to be just right or all their advertising efforts will be a waste.

Enter the function of the three voice adjectives.

GE	Mini
▪ Imaginative	▪ Confident
▪ Responsible	▪ Rebellious
▪ Inspirational	▪ Joyful

With these three defining adjectives, these companies now have a standard to use when creating their packaging and advertisements.

GE can ask:	Mini can ask:
Is it imaginative?	Is it confident?
Is it responsible?	Is it rebellious?
Is it inspirational?	Is it joyful?

Now let's take a look at some ad copy from each company. Using the questions above, can you determine which company is speaking?

1. *Ecomagination*
2. *Plug into the smart gird*
3. *Runs on irregular*
4. *See the world 30% clearer*
5. *Cheetahs are pussies*
6. *Survival of the quickest*
7. *Unleash the possibilities*
8. *NOT NORMAL*
9. *Top down thrills*

(Answers: 1- GE, 2-1 GE, 3-Mini, 4-GE, 5-Mini, 6-Mini, 7-GE, 8-Mini, 9-Mini)

Some of the messaging is quite obvious, such as calling cheetahs pussies. *Very* few companies would venture into that territory, but Mini knows that while someone who buys a Toyota might frown and object when they see that phrase in an ad, their target customer will likely let a rebellious smile sneak out.

Conversely, "unleash the possibilities" may seem like appropriate language for both companies at first glance, but is it more inspirational than rebellious? Yes. When Mini wants to say the same thing it uses language like "top down thrills." It's risky language, but that's exactly what connects them with their target customer, just as responsible language connects GE with theirs.

You hear the voices of companies all around you. Literally. Everywhere.

- Online ads
- Billboards
- TV and print ads
- Radio commercials
- News headlines
- In-store/on-site messaging

Unless you have no contact with society, you have brands talking to you all day. It's a constant broadcast of voice aimed at getting the thousands or millions of target customers to step forward and self-identify.

One thing to note is that you may or may not get your voice right out of the gate. You may think you're targeting men 35-50 only to find out that 9 times out of 10 it's their wives calling you. In cases like that, learn, adjust your voice to speak to your actual audience, and reapproach. It's all part of growing.

Don't be afraid to listen to feedback. How are people hearing about you? What did they hear? What language are they remembering? What words do customers use when they talk to you?

Your voice should speak your customer's language on a peer-to-peer level, and if something works, keep doing it. Familiarity and predictability breed trust. If people are connecting with a phrase, keep using it.

But always, always, always have your three adjectives on display and ask yourself:

Is it . . . . ?
Is it . . . . ?
Is it . . . . ?

Before you know it, customers will be able to recognize your ad copy before they see your logo or your name, just as you can recognize a friend's voice before they turn a corner and walk into sight.

Take note of voices you like and see if they will work for your company. Remember, the voice needs to appeal to your target customer, not necessarily you. If you have a product people take seriously then you need to match your tone to your product. The CEO of Depends may like Mini ads, but that doesn't mean the same voice that sells cars will sell adult underwear protection.

BRAINSTORM TIME

Take a few minutes to list adjectives you want your business to personify. Write down every word that comes to mind. You can narrow down your options later, but to keep the flow going in brainstorm mode you need to let all the words out. You can get picky later.

In the end, you'll want to choose the three strongest adjectives you can realistically maintain, because words with strong meaning will quickly help your audience find you.

VOICE BRAINSTORM

Voice

Brand Promise

Your brand promise is fundamental to your brand's personality. It's what your customer can count on each and *every time* they interact with your brand.

Notice I said every time—not some days or on special days, and not only if you buy the premium model. Every time. Once you create a brand promise, you must deliver on it every time. If something falls outside the scope of your brand promise, then you need to drop it or put it under the umbrella of a different brand. If you don't, people are going to be confused and ultimately disconnect.

Ask yourself: What do you offer all day, every day, with every single product or service? Build your brand promise on that.

AUTHOR PEN NAME

An example of creating multiple entities to target different customers would be an author who decides to take on a second pen name. Let's say there is an author who has made a career writing sweet romances who decides she wants to write something not-so-sweet. What do you think will happen if this author begins publishing her graphic material under the same name as her clean material?

Since this scenario has occurred more than once, not much speculation is needed on what happens when an author keeps the same name for these value-opposite genres. It's disastrous. The "clean" readers feel betrayed when they're tricked into buying explicit material, and readers who want graphic scenes feel tricked when they buy a book with only one kiss tacked on at the end.

The backlash from both audiences is universal, the reviews are abysmal, and sales disappear. Both audiences have lost trust, and the author's options are to either retire or make up a new name and start all over.

BRAINSTORM TIME

Regardless of your business category, you can expect strong reactions when you betray a brand promise—whether the brand is an actual business or simply the branding of your name, it doesn't matter. What matters is the brand promise your customer can trust you to deliver every time.

Put some time into your brand promise and identify what your customers can count on you bringing to the table each and every time they interact with you.

Once you've decided what your brand promise is, be prepared to advertise and deliver it.

BRAND PROMISES

Brand
Promise

Values

Your values shape your business personality and directly inform your brand promise. Your values show others what's important in your world.

Take a moment to think of companies you love and why you love them. What values are they built on that resonate with you?

Do the same exercise with companies you hate. What values are they built on that rub you wrong?

Look around at the brands surrounding you at this very moment. Your phone, your computer, any food or drink items you have with you. What brands are you currently wearing and what car do you drive?

What values are infused into the brands you love that make you a loyal customer?

- Are they high quality?
- Are they made locally?
- Are they always affordable?
- All they all-natural?
- Do they do one thing the competition doesn't?

- Do they look better?
- Are they more comfortable?
- Do they last forever?
- Do they keep their shape/color?
- Do they support up-and-coming talent?

The list can go on and on, but if you are loyal to a brand, chances are they do one thing really well that you like. That's a brand value.

What's your brand's value?

TOMS

Toms sells shoes. That's their product (among others), but it's not what Toms is selling. What Toms is really selling is the value behind their brand promise of "one for one," which promises that every time you buy a pair of their shoes, Toms will donate a second pair to a child in need.

Yes, you can get similar shoes from a competitor for cheaper, but that competitor isn't going to gift a new pair of shoes to a child in need.

Toms is a great illustration as to how the values of your business can create customer loyalty because it underscores how your company's core values can be either industry- or community-related. You can be like Chipotle, a company committed to the quality of life their animals enjoy before they become part of the menu, or you can be like Lady Gaga and be highly dedicated to a social cause outside of your industry. Either approach or a combination of the two can be successful, so long as they are consistent.

BRANDY MELVILLE

Brandy Melville is a brand of girls' clothing that only sells up to size Small (size 2). Their value system embraces only the petite.

This level of exclusivity based solely on a girl's size gets a lot of push back from those who fight against an anorexic culture, but loyal customers see things differently. They see cute, affordable clothing that keeps them on trend. They love Brandy Melville's offering and are unfazed by the knowledge that anyone with a circumference larger than 25 inches need not apply. That's fine with them. Those people can shop somewhere else.

In this case, Brandy Melville's values are met with opposite reactions—one enthusiastic and the other a soap box of opposition. If you truly stand for something then you are likely going to create a similar split reaction in public opinion.

HARLEY-DAVIDSON

Another example of brand values is Harley-Davidson, a company that vocally supports troops on active duty. But do they just put a yellow ribbon in their shop window and call that support? No. In most cases, locations take their support a step further by offering free motorcycle storage to any deployed soldier who has bought a Harley from their location. This is a *huge* savings and a business value that nearly everyone can get behind. And those who are not behind it are probably a bit jealous that they don't qualify for free storage themselves.

BRAINSTORM TIME

Examining the values of other companies can

help you better identify the values you want your company to embrace.

Reflect on the brands that currently have your loyalty. What have those brands done to make you feel so confident in supporting them?

Once you feel comfortable that you understand the values that resonate with you, it's time to craft your own. Start with up to three value statements you are willing and able to take action on.

P!nk is a singer/songwriter by profession, but she is also a committed vegan who uses performance art to communicate why being a vegan is important to her. Similarly, Josh Duhamel is an actor who quietly volunteers at animal shelters when he is touring through a city to promote a film.

Think like Toms, Brandy Melville, Harley-Davidson, P!nk, and Josh Duhamel. What values can you embody in your business that customers can applaud you for. Where are you willing to take action beyond simple lip service and lead by example without flip-flopping and betraying trust in the future?

As a brand you don't need to be all things to

all people. You just need to be authentic, which means your values should be authentic. People can smell a poser from a mile away so don't aim to pander. Stick to your own truth and make it your value-based rallying cry.

💡 IMMUTABLE VALUES

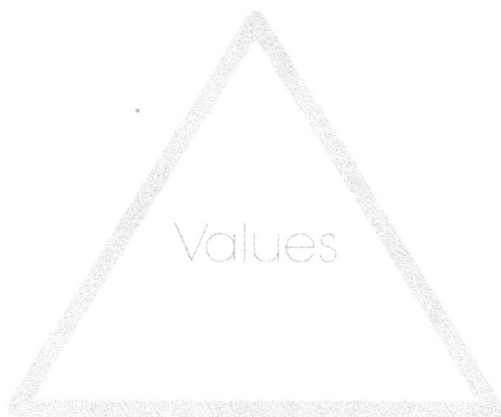

Your Industry

A huge part of branding is understanding the market and your place it.

- Who are your competitors?
- How are they positioned in the field?
- How do you compare to them?
- Who's more expensive?
- Who's cheaper?
- What are your competitors doing better than you?
- What do you do better than your competition?

It can be easy to pretend that your peers are not worthy of your study, but doing so is the equivalent of a sports team refusing to play games against other teams and self-proclaiming that they are the undisputed division champions.

It doesn't work that way. Teams practice, coaches watch tapes of other teams, and rivals face off against each other to see who earns bragging rights. Both teams bring their A-games, but in the end the stats add up showing who is the winner.

Study the competition. Know their plays and have your own plan. Go head-to-head with the competition and see how you fare. And if you need help connecting with customers who are currently with the competition then take things a step further and take a look at how and where your competitors are connecting with customers.

What social media sites have a lot of traction?

Where do their ads show up?

What do their loyal customers like about them?

Find the moves that are working and add them to your playbook. There's no reason to reinvent the wheel if one is there for the taking. Are there any free lessons you can pick up from the competition, or is there a blind spot where you can own the space?

To truly compete, you need to know your industry inside out.

- Who is your strongest competition?
- Which brand is the best-value in your industry?
- What is the total revenue of your industry?
- What is your share within the industry?

- What are the company values of your greatest competitor?
- What makes you unique in your field?

Perform some research and learn current answers to these questions. Then stay up-to-date with the data as it evolves. If it's relevant to your industry, it's relevant to your business and your brand and you should know it.

BRAINSTORM TIME

Take a few minutes to answer each of the questions mentioned in this section in order to get a sense of your industry and your place within it.

ALL ABOUT YOUR INDUSTRY

Industry

Experience

Experience breeds trust. It's the reason consumers check tags and labels on products. They want to know if they can trust the brand to be what they need.

Think about all the products in your home and how you trust them to perform their functions. From your dish soap and your washer, to your couch and TV, everything you own has a reputation for quality, or lack thereof, in the marketplace based on the experience it provides. It's the reason some bicycles are $50 and some are $5,000.

So what experience do *you* bring to your field? What credentials are valued? Your customer will definitely care.

Are you an architect who earned a high degree and has since won several industry awards, or are you a parent who desperately needed a product for your child and invented it out of necessity? Whether your experience is industry validated or won in the school of hard knocks, it has merit and your customers need to see it.

Going back to the TV series *The Shark Tank*, you will notice that experience is something the sharks ask about every time.

- Who are you?
- What's the story behind the product?
- Why are you the best one to move your business into the future?

The answers to these questions alone can make or break a deal with investors and customers.

Imagine a man who claims to have invented the perfect road bicycle. The inventor doesn't actually cycle himself and has no reputable cyclists vouching for his design, but he promises it is still the best bike on the market.

Now put this guy's bike next to the bike that just won the *Tour de France*. When the *Tour de France* winner points to his bike and says it's the best, and the inventor points to his bike and says it's the best, who are you going to believe?

These showdowns of credibility happen every day in the business world. Your experience creates a product that your customers experience, and that customer experience creates your reputation. Your industry experience directly informs your customer experience. This is why your experience in your field carries so much weight.

When you create a reputation for using your experience to provide both a consistent and positive customer experience, shoppers and clients gain security in the predictability you provide.

Think of Starbucks. Do they make the best coffee in the world? Pretty much every poll ever taken says no, they don't. Yet they are by far the largest coffee chain.

Why?

Consistency and experience.

Starbucks may not be the best, but if you're going to drop $5 for a coffee, you at least want to be confident you won't hate it, right? So while Starbucks may not be high-end luxury coffee, if you see their sign in New York, Dubai, or Shanghai, you know what you're going to get, and there's comfort in that.

Starbucks doesn't have to serve the best coffee to be #1 in the coffee business. They just need to be the best at delivering an experience the on-the-go customer wants to repeat.

Your experience in your field will have a direct impact on your customer's experience with your product or service. Experience speaks to you credentials and your competencies, which is why customers and investors alike will always ask you about it.

BRAINSTORM TIME

What experience do you have in your field, and what credibility or tactical advantage does it give you?

YOUR EXPERIENCE

PERSONALITY CONCLUSION

Just as there is more to you than what you can do and how you look, there is more to your brand than what you sell and the package you put it in.

As much as anything, your brand is about the personality and attitude you bring to your industry. People may initially choose your product or service simply because you look like the basic fit they need, but the loyal customer relationship comes when there is a personality click—when you become the brand that isn't just hocking wares for maximum profit. Loyalty comes with trust, shared values, and vision.

So don't shy away from creating a culture for your company that people can get to know and even join. Develop your brand personality and let it shine. Doing so will attract the kind of clients (and employees) you want.

Once you have established both the foundation and the personality of your brand, you will be able to use them to design the more visible aspects of your brand in the style section.

Right now your pyramid should look like this:

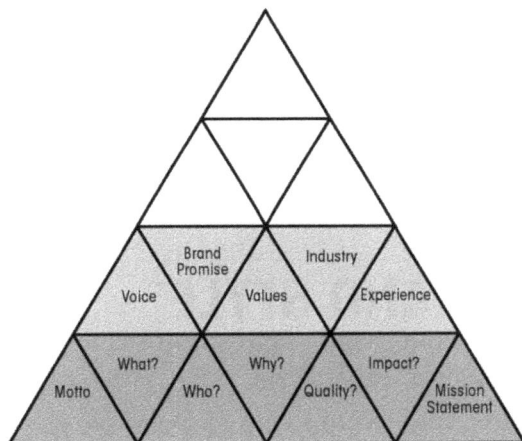

YOUR BRAND STYLE

The Style tier addresses how your brand is seen in the world. I like to refer to it as the hair, makeup, and wardrobe of branding. If you know who you are and what you want, then you should know how to dress for success.

The same goes for your company, and your third tier is focused on making sure your brand looks the part. Doing that requires adopting and maintaining a consistent style.

Your Tagline

Earlier we discussed the difference between a motto and a tagline. As a reminder:

- A motto is an internal employee mantra

- A tagline (or slogan) is an external marketing tool that helps people connect to your brand

A tagline is a snapshot of your brand experience—what people can expect when they choose you.

Your tagline should also encapsulate your company spirit defined in your Personality tier.

If you're a playful brand, your tagline should be playful. If you're sentimental, be sentimental. If you're serious, be serious. But whatever you do, aim at evoking positive emotion. How people feel about your tagline directly impacts how they feel about your brand, so be careful about going dark with your language.

As you consider potential taglines, it's good to note that taglines are rarely an actual sentence. More often they are a catchy phrase that creates the promise of a desirable customer experience. Some taglines examples from large companies include:

Mazda: Zoom-zoom
Toyota: Let's go places
Coca-Cola: Open happiness

Dr. Pepper: Always one of a kind

Each tagline transports you into the brand's world for just a moment. With Mazda, you're joyfully speeding; with Toyota, you're on an adventure; with Coca-Cola, you're happy; and with Dr. Pepper you're special.

Earlier we discussed how in a taste test 50% of participants chose Pepsi for flavor, but 75% of participants said they would still buy Coke. Why is that? Well, I'll go out on a limb and say that this seemingly irrational dynamic may be created in part by Pepsi's inability to create a brand personality that can be expressed in a memorable and compelling tagline.

Out of curiosity, can you think of Pepsi's current slogan off the top of your head?

Unless you're a diehard, you probably can't. And even if you can recall their current slogan, you may be confused by the fact that you have multiple current options to choose from. This multiplicity of taglines muddies the branding waters and leaves people uncertain of what a product stands for. And when people are uncertain about your tagline, they are uncertain about your brand in general.

Unfortunately, Pepsi is a perfect example of a company running multiple vague campaigns rather than one compelling campaign. But I would bet you money that if they finally hit their sweet spot with a slogan their sales would jump.

Successful taglines are as recognizable as a company's logo. For example, reading the words JUST DO IT almost certainly brings a company name and logo into your mind without you even having to stop to think about it. Someone says "JUST DO IT" and you say "Nike." Someone says "Nike" and you say "JUST DO IT." Someone shows you their swoosh logo and you say "Nike—JUST DO IT."

That's impeccably strong branding.

It's highly improbable that you're reading this book because you anticipate overtaking Nike in brand recognition, but you don't need to. All you need to do is attract your target demographic by briefly taking them into your world and letting them know there is room for them there.

👍 FAMILIAR TAGLINES

Based on their taglines alone, which company is most likely to have a product or service you want to experience?

Have it your way — Burger King

What happens here, stays here — Las Vegas

There are some things money can't buy. For everything else, there's Mastercard — Mastercard

Think different — Apple

Mmm Mmm good — Campbell's Soup

Ladies and gentlemen serving ladies and gentlemen — Ritz-Carlton

Double your pleasure, double your fun — Wrigley's Doublemint

Are you in good hands? — Allstate

Which of these taglines appeals to you the most? How does it make you feel? And if you recall that slogan the next time you see the product in the store, do you think the positive emotion it brings to mind may impact your willingness to give the brand a try?

Most people do.

BRAINSTORM TIME

No matter how small you are, a strong brand tagline has merit. It tells people how to feel about you, and when they know how to feel about you, they know if they like you. If you can take them to places they want to share with others, then you have just created a brand ambassador through the use of a few words, and every company needs that.

Take a few moments to identify unique experiences you provide and the emotions that may result. If your brand is a cleaning solution, you're not selling a bottle of liquid. You're selling the sensation of living in a pristine environment. If your company makes golf balls, you're not selling a ball. You're selling the victory of a perfect shot.

What experience are you bringing to your customer, and what feelings do you invite into their world?

Don't try to come up with a perfect tagline out of the gate. Just start writing things down. Get it all down and refine later. Give yourself permission to be messy.

TAGLINE BRAINSTORM

Tagline

Your Company Name

When you were born, your parents gave you a name. Throughout your life, you have developed a reputation for that name. Now, when others hear your name, their experiences with you jump to mind and create their impression of who you are. Are you punctual? Do you smell good? Are you wise? Do you have a great smile?

Answers to these questions are your (often unspoken) social brand.

Celebrities take personal branding to a whole new level by creating reputations that either attract or repel consumers based on the experience they create. Celebrities are not famous because everybody loves them. They are famous because everyone knows what to expect from them.

NAME RECOGNITION

Pay attention to how you feel as you read the following names: Ellen Degeneres, Justin Timberlake, Beyoncé, Bruce Lee, Muhatma

Gandhi, Justin Bieber, Oprah Winfrey, Princess Diana, Tyler Perry, Angelina Jolie, Maya Angelou.

Each of the names you recognize on this list should create an emotional response in you. The important difference to note between a celebrity name and an everyday name, however, is that the way you feel about celebrity names is no accident. The reputation and experiences surrounding each celebrity name is carefully projected out into the public by people who know they don't have to please everyone. They just need to please people who want the brand experience.

As a business, you will create similar intentional impressions using your business name. The experiences people have with your brand name should be conscious, strategic, and—above all—predictable. People don't visit a business or buy a product because they want to be surprised. They dish out the money to get exactly what they want. Your brand name should communicate the quality and value your customers can expect, but also their experience.

Choose Your Baggage Carefully

Like a celebrity, your brand might be your legal name. It might also be a *nom de plume* or a more conventional business name. Whatever you choose, it's important to note the baggage that comes along with the words or names you choose.

For example, choosing to rebrand the name Hitler isn't wise because it's very unlikely that you will do anything more impactful than the Hitler who made the name (in)famous. This is an extreme example of a general principle: Names and words have histories and hues to them. Use these histories and hues to your advantage and make changes where needed.

If your name is Vlad Dommer and you want to be the next Nicholas Sparks, you have a name problem. If you want to be the next Martha Stewart and your name is Vickie Hooker, you have a name problem. And if you are a weight-loss coach who has named your business Sweet Success, you have a name problem.

Creating a brand means that you don't have to make a given name work. You can choose a name and put it to work. So be objective. Use words and names to your benefit. Don't fight or try to redefine them.

👍 MARILYN MANSON

When a shock rocker by the name of Brian Hugh Warner decided to go big with his industrial metal band, he chose to define himself using the juxtaposition of two very different iconic names: Marilyn Monroe and Charles Manson. The first is the name of a silver screen icon, and the second is one of the most dangerously charismatic cult leaders of the twentieth century.

At first the name is confusing and uncomfortable as you subconsciously put Marilyn Monroe and Charles Manson in the same headspace. Your brain doesn't like that, so you feel compelled to search out who the real Marilyn Manson is. And when you see Marilyn Manson, he pretty much fits the disconcerting mental image you were seeking to banish from your mind. It's a guy named Marilyn wearing clown-levels of eerie makeup and singing music you might expect to hear at a cult-like gathering. You take one glance at Marilyn Manson's carefully crafted look and say, "Yep. That's about what I was expecting." And from that moment on you know who Marilyn Manson is. Whether you listen to his music or not, once you see him you can pick him out of a rocker lineup without hesitation.

But would you remember Brian Hugh Warner? No. You wouldn't. In fact, you probably already forgot about him.

From beginning to end, Marilyn Manson works as a brand name because it puts existing names to work in an unforgettable way.

Be Memorable

Marilyn Manson is a memorable name, and your name should be too. But maybe your parents didn't give you a memorable name, or maybe someone famous is already using your name. Maybe your name is laden with unfortunate innuendo or flat-out hard to say. These are all branding concerns.

There is a fun trick you can use when

choosing brand names, logos, and taglines. Present people with options and ask them what their favorites are. Then come back to those people three days later and see if they can remember which name they chose.

Can they? And if not, can they remember any of the other options?

In the end, the options people remember should get double votes—maybe even triple votes. Liking something is nice and all, but think about how many things you like online in a given day. Can you recall even half of them 24 hours later?

In the end, you're not looking for your brand to be something nice or cute or likeable. You need your brand to be memorable. So if people who love you can't remember things they've claimed to like, a stranger definitely isn't going to remember them.

Aim for memorable with all your choices.

Your Name, Brand Name, or Nom de Plume?

There's no standard right or wrong answer as

to what you should name your business. There's only the answer you want to live with day in and day out. Each option has pros and cons.

Type	Pro	Con
Your Name	Creates built-in advertising	You cannot pick and choose personal experiences people associate with your brand.
Nom de plume	Provides increased privacy while still seeming personal	People have a hard enough time remembering one name, not to mention your second name.
Brand Name	Increases professional appearance	Consumers have expectations of formal companies which will require a greater investment in a professional image.

If you look around you will find compelling arguments for each naming option. People are happy to share what has worked for them. It is for you to decide which approach is the best fit for you.

BRAND NAME OPTIONS

Brand
Name

Style Guide

You see style guides at work all day, every day. Whether you consciously know what a style guide is or not, chances are that you can fill in some of the basics on popular brands.

Style guides create visual cues using colors, fonts, layouts, and other details to let you know who you're dealing with at a glance. Large brands use the same colors, fonts, and logo placement on their products and marketing to an obsessive degree.

VISUAL STYLES

Before we discuss elements in your style guide, see how well you can recognize style elements of well-known companies. Complete each of the following activities to show how visual cues in advertisements reinforce branding and brand recognition.

Following are three screen grabs from advertisements for three competing shipping companies: UPS, FedEx, and DHL. Without seeing the logo, can you identify which ad belongs to which brand? (Note: Those of you who are viewing this on a full-color e-reader have an advantage of seeing colors here, but even if you are seeing the images in black and white, still give this exercise a stab by looking for other style guide elements that cue you in to which company is which.)

UPS   FedEx   DHL

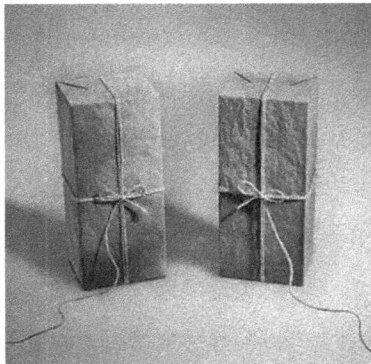

UPS   FedEx   DHL

UPS   FedEx   DHL

The images may be generic, but when a color scheme is applied to them, your mind quickly connects the dots, saving you the effort of reading through content to learn who and what the ad is about. Colors do a lot of heavy lifting in the branding game. If you doubt it, go to a sports game and observe the role and power of colors.

Wherever there is competition, colors matter. So take care when you choose your colors. Be strategic, and then be consistent. Use the same colors every time. Because every time you change the hue in the slightest, people have to relearn how to spot you in the fray, and there's no guarantee they're going to do you that service.

You need to do it for them with your style guide.

What Style Guides Accomplish

Style guides help customers and competition recognize you by sight. The more consistent you are, the more recognizable you are.

Creating a style guide includes defining things like the exact shades of colors that will be used in everything the public sees. It means selecting what fonts you will use as well as when and where each font is used. It means matching your business cards to your website so your customer doesn't need to do any additional mental processing to conclude that they're at the right website once they've arrived.

It means creating the most predictable visual experience possible for your customer.

When you create a style guide, you will probably get a bit of a headache and feel like there is just too much to process. If you experience this, my advice is to stop and feel the mental frustration you're experience and think, *Filtering unbranded materials down to branded materials is a lot of mental work, which I am currently requiring my visitors to do for me. But once I define a style and implement it, neither me nor my* customers will every have to think about it again, which means we can all think about other things.

Large companies are *very* nitpicky about style guides because they understand that a flicker of frustration in a customer can result in the loss of a sale. They know that the mind sees in pictures, not it words. And when the pictures and the details—even details as small as font type sizing, space ratios, and element locations—need to be reprocessed with each new exposure, there is a good chance potential customers will decide to eject and go somewhere else that requires less work.

This is why strong brands obsess over where design elements are placed, the exact colors used, the transparency applied, the size and font of text elements, the spatial relationships between elements, and every other seemingly obsessive detail.

Imagine the care with which a Kardashian checks herself in the mirror before leaving for a red carpet event, and you'll have a sense of the scrutiny ads and packaging go through in a large company. Although the end result might look effortless, it is anything but.

Branding is about creating predictable experiences on every level—including a visual level. To accomplish that, you need clearly define standards that are not only recognizable from across the room, but also across mediums.

Doing so starts with little things as small as a font.

Font

Fonts are a little-talked-about secret weapon in branding. When a font is off, most people can't put their finger on it. Going back to the metaphor of your brand style being like its hair, makeup, and wardrobe, when an established font suddenly goes off brand, it's like seeing a woman who forgot to put on mascara or who borrowed a different shade of lipstick. Something is off and everyone sees it, but unless you're tuned in to cosmetics, you may not be able to pinpoint what is different.

The same goes for fonts. Unless you're working in a field that requires and eye for typesetting, you may not realize how tuned in you actually are to the proportions, weights, and spacing of fonts. You may not know what *serif* and *san serif* mean, but the second someone points out the difference (This is a serif font. This is a san serif font.), you'll clearly see what you've been seeing all along.

When I point out that research shows that san serif is easier to read on screens, you'll suddenly notice how nearly ever website you visit has san serif fonts, like Arial or Calibri. And when I point out that, for some reason, serif fonts are easier to read on printed materials, like pages of a book, you'll suddenly notice that nearly every book you pick up uses a serif font, like Times New Roman or Book Antiqua.

Serif on a book page; san serif on a web page.

Your eyes expect to see both all the time, which means you only really notice a website or book's font when they break the best practice. When this happens, there is even the chance that the wrong font in the wrong place will bother you enough to make you distrust the information or its source. Your brain knows something is off, but only someone with trained eyes will be thinking, *This guy is trying to stand out by putting serif text on his website, which adds weight to the letters and makes my eyes work harder and read slower. Because of the increased difficulty of reading serif font on a screen, I have less mental energy to dedicate to processing the information he's giving me which makes me want to stop reading and move on even though this is actually good information.*

Most of us are not that self-aware of our motives when we find a font agitating or out of place. All we know is that something is different and we don't like it.

This is just one of many reasons why most businesses apply a font style guide to all their public materials. Consistent fonts help create a consistent experience, even on a serif/san serif level.

FAMILIAR FONTS

Using only the fonts as a cue, can you correctly match each advertising message to Nike, Reebok, or Adidas?

DON'T PUSH BOUNDARIES, BREAK THROUGH THEM

Nike   Reebok   Adidas

GIVE ME WHERE TO STAND AND I WILL MOVE THE EARTH.

Nike   Reebok   Adidas

CHOOSE.

Nike   Reebok   Adidas

The fonts all look similar, right? Each company is using an ALL CAPS, san serif approach in each example, yet the fonts have different weights and angles. The differences may seem small, but your eyes see them and learn to correctly associate them so your brain can think about other things.

Use your gut to choose which font belongs to which brand, then check to see if you're right. I'm betting you are.

(Answers: 1=Reebok, 2=Nike, 3=Adidas)

BRAINSTORM TIME

To reinforce your branding efforts, consciously choose a font style guide for each of the following content categories, and stick with them:

Title text:

Header text:

Subheader text:

Body text:

Disclaimer text:

Tagline text:

You don't need a custom font or anything special. You can stick the usual fonts you see every day or variations of them. The goal here is not to be glaringly different. The goal is to be consistent and keep the typeface, proportions, and sizes the same so that mental pictures line up in your customer's mind.

☼ YOUR COMPANY FONTS

Style
Guide

Choosing Your Color Palette

Just like Superman and Batman identify with a specific color palette, so should you.

Few things are so universal across time as people identifying with color palettes. Whether that is in the form of a coat of arms, a flag, a military uniform, royalty, religion, education, or sports teams doesn't matter. For as long as we have a documented history, colors matter.

This means the colors you choose for your brand matter and should stay as constant as the colors of your favorite school or sports team.

Your company's colors can identify you at a glance, even from a distance. Your mind doesn't have to work too hard to tell whether that's the Hulk, Iron Man, or Captain America on the screen during an Avengers movie, and that's because of the style guides applied to each character—not the least of which is their distinct color palette.

Captain America and Iron Man may both have red in their costumes, but it's a different red. Thor and the Hulk may both have big muscles, but you could definitely tell them apart from a hundred yards away based on color alone.

It should be just as easy to distinguish you from your competitors, and color is one of the style tools you can use to stand apart from the competitor standing next to you.

> Do some research on colors to make sure you are using shades and colors that reinforce your values and messaging by researching color meanings and the history of colors.

COLOR PALETTES

Branded businesses have official color palettes that must be used in all branded materials. View some well-known examples below, and notice how they vary from very simple to more elaborate. Either approach is fine, but it is important that the direction is constant and unchanging.

WORDPRESS

	Blue		Orange		Grey
	Pantone 7468		Pantone 1655		Pantone Black 7
	CMYK 97, 44, 26, 3		CMYK 6, 86, 100, 1		CMYK 65, 60, 60, 45
	Hex #21759b		Hex #d54e21		Hex #464846
	RGB 33, 117, 155		RGB 213, 78, 33		RGB 70, 70, 70

Source: https://wordpress.org/about/logos/

(Search "**brand color palettes**" at www.wickedsassy.com
to see these images in full color.)

DROPBOX

Source: https://www.dropbox.com/branding

EBAY

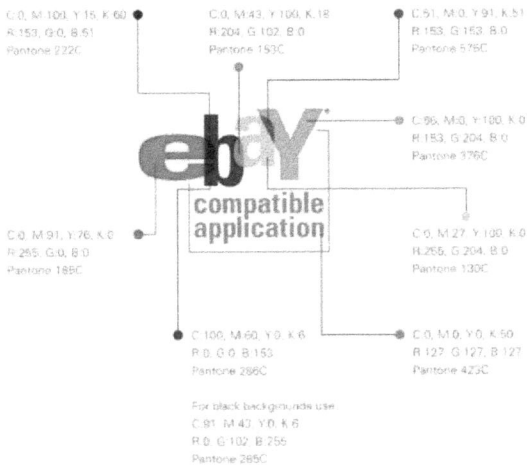

Source: http://developer.ebay.com/join/logo/logoguidelines.pdf

ADOBE

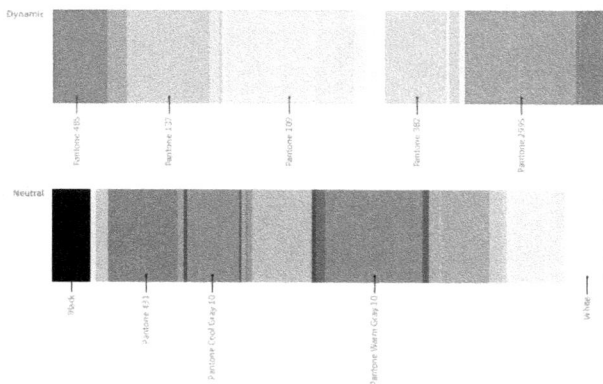

Dynamic

Pantone 485 | Pantone 137 | Pantone 109 | Pantone 180 | Pantone 2995

Neutral

Black | Pantone 431 | Pantone Cool Gray 10 | Pantone Warm Gray 10 | White

MAILCHIMP

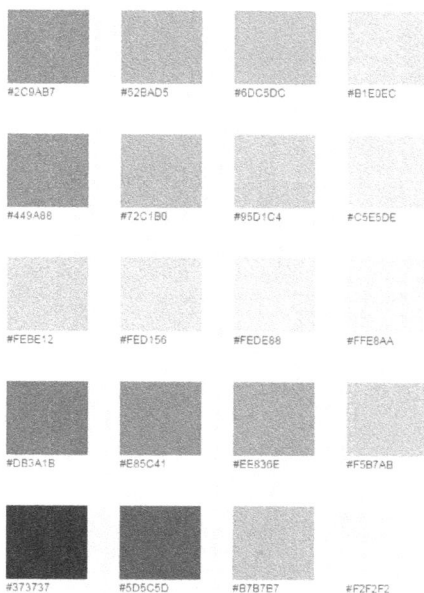

#2C9AB7	#52BAD5	#6DC5DC	#B1E3EC
#449A88	#72C1B0	#95D1C4	#C5E5DE
#FEBE12	#FED156	#FEDE88	#FFE8AA
#DB3A1B	#E85C41	#EE836E	#F5B7AB
#373737	#5D5C5D	#B7B7B7	#F2F2F2

BRAINSTORM TIME

It's time to choose your brand colors. You'll need:

- Neutral tones
- Identifying colors
- Accent colors

Once you choose colors, you'll need to document the exact shade and/or code for that color. There are several options to do this for free online by googling: *color palette maker*. Most of the people I work with like to use the free online color wheel from Adobe, but choose whichever tools work best for you.

At minimum, you will need to define the following colors (RGB, CMYK, Hex, PMS, Pantone):

Neutral Color #1: *Probably black—used for text, etc.*

Neutral Color #2: *Possibly a shade of gray used for subtle visual offsetting*

Neutral Color #3: *Usually white (background)*

Brand Color #1: *If you were a sports team, what color would your jersey be?*

Brand Color #2: *What is a secondary color on your team's jersey?*

Brand Color #3: (optional): *Is there a third prominent color that would be visible on your jersey?*

Accent Color #1: *What is your call to action color (e.g., Buy button color)?*

Pick colors you like then wait 72 hours and see if you still like them. Then test the colors on others to see their reactions. Third-party input is important, because if you do things right, loyal customers will wear your colors—but only if they like them. If they hate the colors, they'll wear your branded material next time they have to paint a wall.

So do both you and your customer a favor and choose colors you both want to wear in public.

☀ YOUR COLOR PALETTE

Style
Guide

Creating Comfort with Layouts

Predictability builds trust, and trust builds a brand. This means *everything* related to your brand should be as predictable as possible—the placement of your logo, the format of your prices, the display of your offerings.

Everything.

PRODUCT LAYOUTS

We see the layouts of large brands so often that they eventually become cultural visual staples. It's like how you are reading the words in this book from left-to-right, line-by-line without thinking about it. At one point you painstakingly learned how to read, but now reading is intuitive. It's a learned cultural skill that helps you navigate the world more easily.

In many cases, we interact with brands on this same familiar level. When we have repetitive exposures to their layouts and style guides, our minds accept the pattern as "natural," and we look for it—like we would look for spots on a leopard or feathers on a peacock.

For example, imagine this rectangle is an Apple laptop. Where does the logo go?

Here's another rectangle. Pretend it's a Visa credit card. Where does the Visa logo go?

Now pretend you are buying something on Amazon. Where is the *Buy* button?

The predictability of all of these placements is something your mind takes for granted until someone switches things up.

- Imagine consumer reactions if Apple started putting its logo on the top-left corner of products.
- Imagine if Visa put their logo only on the back of a credit card.
- Imagine if Amazon moved its *Buy* button to the bottom of every page and made you scroll down anytime you wanted to make a purchase.

Each of these choices would cause confusion and probably even outrage, which is why they won't happen. Each of these companies has firm style guides and they're sticking to them.

Your customers should have similar predictability when working with you. They should expect to see your branding, and they should know exactly where they should expect to see it.

In short, they should be able to recognize you as easily as they can recognize a leopard or peacock.

Just like you know where to look for a

Starbucks logo on a coffee cup, your customers should know where and when your logo will make an appearance and be correct 100% of the time. This consistent predictability creates trust.

To this end, you need firm instructions for where and when your logo is used, and where visual elements and messaging belong on any item. You customer shouldn't have to work to find you. You need to do the work for them so they can identify you at a glance.

BRAINSTORM TIME

As you establish your style guide, you will need to think about where and how you want to use your logo. Remember, this is the face of your business, so if you are creating a customer experience, you want your logo in sight.

Create a style guide for when and how your logo should be used. Where does it go on:

- Products
- Printed material
- Your website
- Your business cards
- Vehicles

- Advertisements
- Anything else your customer sees

Map out acceptable placements of your logo in diagrams you can share with anyone so that the decisions are pre-made and consistent. Because if you don't have to think about where to put your logo, your customers don't have to think about where to find it.

SKETCH IT OUT (LAYOUT)

Style
Guide

STYLE CONCLUSION

The branding elements in your Style tier are the tools you use to stand out in a crowd. It's the difference between Spider-man and the Green Lantern. It's the difference between Lex Luthor and the Joker. It's the difference between Netflix and Hulu.

- Your name gives people an immediate taste for your business. Choose it with care.
- Your tagline projects your personality into the marketplace. Keep it authentic.
- Your fonts create subtle consistency while giving people a hint of a personality. Keep them consistent.
- Your colors give a sense of your spirit. Choose colors you and your customers can proudly wear in public.
- Your layouts determine how quickly and easily people identify your brand. Help people identify you at a glance 100% of the time through your consistency.

Every element of Your Style tier is visible to the world at large, so choose these brand details in advance and stay true to your style guide.

And if the day comes when you need to make a change, do it holistically, boldly, and carry nothing over. No cross pollinating the old and the new. Rebranding is like a nose job. You can't keep the old and have the new at the same time. You have to choose and make the leap.

Once you've chosen each of these elements, your brand foundation, personality, and style will be established, and you'll be ready to run full speed ahead into designing the face of your company.

YOUR COMPANY FACE: THE ALMIGHTY LOGO

At last, we reach the top of the pyramid and the face of your company: Your logo.

SAY IT IN PICTURES

As mentioned in the style guide, humans are visual creatures. If I asked you if you know John, you would likely hesitate before answering. There are a lot of Johns in the world. We might be thinking of the same guy, we might not.

But if I held up a picture of a man's face and asked you if you knew him, your answer would likely come more quickly and with more confidence.

People don't think in words. We think in pictures. This is why one name can bring multiple faces to mind. John may be a specific name, but it is also a category for *Men Named John* in your mind.

When you brand, your job is to create an identity where people think of a general category, like John, and immediately think of you.

MAKE 1+1= YOU

If you want people to think specifically, you need to provide them with a specific image they can pull up each and every time they hear your brand name. The quicker they pull up a "face," the stronger your brand recognition.

There are several men with the name Brad Pitt, but one face will likely jump to mind when you hear that name. Why? Because Brad Pitt has been branded. It would take a whole lot of interaction with one of the other Brad Pitts for you to replace the image of the celebrity Brad Pitt as your default image attached to the name.

However, if you hear the name *Brad* all by

itself, your mind might bring up a friend or no face at all. It's like saying *hamburger*. Maybe you think of one hamburger in particular; maybe your mind brings up hamburger as a category; or maybe you visually recall every hamburger you've ever seen in the order you saw them. Same goes with *Pitt* or *pit*. That label could mean any number of things, so your mind hesitates on pinpointing one result as the "right" result.

But when you put the two terms together:

Brad + Pitt = One image rising to the top with no real visual competition

This is branding.

Use What Comes Naturally

This same general-to-specific visual recognition occurs when someone hears your business name. If all a customer knows is your name, recognition might be iffy. It would be like asking them if they know Brad. But if they can connect your name to a mental image they've seen multiple times, people will recall your brand more quickly and confidently.

Don't believe me? Look at the list of

companies below. Which companies do you know, and what image comes to mind as you read the name?

- Disney
- Warner Brothers
- Pixar
- Bad Robot
- DreamWorks
- Castle Rock Entertainment

Did you know some companies better than others? How long did you have to look at each name before you could confidently identify your familiarity or lack of familiarity with it? What was the image that came to mind that helped you identify the company? Was it a logo or a moment from a movie?

Whatever came to mind, I'm betting it was an image or a series of images, and not words.

The recall process you just used to think about the list of production companies is the same process people will use to bring your brand to mind when someone mentions your brand name. They'll search for an image. They won't remember words or lettering. They'll remember images, experiences, and emotions and the faces they attach to each.

Your logo is the face of experiences you create. It's how you are recognized by peers and customers alike. You need to use this face to create the visual recognition process that helps people pick you out of the trillion other things they have stored in their brain and say, "Oh, yeah. I know them."

Logos Should Give You Room to Grow

Your logo does not need to be a literal representation of who you are and what you do. All the image needs to do is be true to the rest of your brand pyramid—especially your Voice, Values, and Mission Statement.

Before setting out to create the logo for your company, look around at the logos all around you.

Is McDonald's logo a picture of food?

Is Microsoft's logo a picture of a computer?

Is Verizon's logo a picture of a phone?

The purpose of a logo is not to identify the industry you work in. The purpose of your logo is to create a face for your company that is harmonious with your brand promise.

That said, there also nothing wrong with having a literal image as a logo, especially if you are a small business. If you're a new cupcake shop, then having a cupcake in your logo isn't the worst idea ever. People will look at your logo and immediately know you sell cupcakes. But if you ever grow to the point that you make other baked items as well, the logo might hinder your growth because everyone just sees you as the cupcake shop. It doesn't occur to them to buy a birthday cake from you.

So as you create your logo, take care that you do not approve an image that limits future growth. Your logo should visually capture your values and add to your credibility.

Logo Qualities

Your logo should be:
- Eye catching
- Memorable
- Easy to describe
- Easy to stencil or embroider
- Something you want on your body (shirts, hats, etc.)

- A design that prints well on packaging
- Discernible from 10 feet away

Make Sure Your Logo Fits Into the Family

You should never copy a competitor's logo, but your logo should look like it belongs in your industry. Do a search to find the logos of the top five or ten companies in your industry, then put their logos all on one page.

As you look at your competitors' logos, ask yourself this question: How can you fit in while simultaneously standing out?

SOCIAL MEDIA

To illustrate this concept of blending in while standing out, let's take a look at some branded social media icons you likely see every day.

Most pages you visit online will have buttons similar to these available—simple, visual buttons that help you share content. Now ask yourself:

- Do these icons look like they belong together?
- Can you tell them apart?

There are only six icons in the example, but look at them closely. Notice the use of color, font, and layout. Three of the buttons are predominantly blue, and three are red. (If you are seeing these images in color on a device like a Kindle or a Nook, you can also see that none of the blues or reds are the same shade between the companies. If you are looking at the icons in black and white you can see that even without color differentiators each icon stands apart visually, while looking like it belongs.) The style guides for these companies are so strong that each icon is easily identified based on the font alone.

Your logo should fit into the other brands of your industry in a similar fashion.

The Red Carpet Test

I like to apply what I call the Red Carpet test to any logo.

Pretend there is a huge event for something you care about. Maybe it's a fund raiser for a nonprofit or a huge event for your favorite sport. Maybe it's a film festival or a local race. Whatever the event may be, you have chosen to sponsor it as a company.

As part of your sponsorship, the event is displaying your logo on banners for the event's red carpet or podium. You're not the only sponsor. A local TV station is sponsoring the event, as is a radio station, and several other large businesses in your area—all your logos placed together to form a wallpaper backdrop for the event.

Does your logo fit in?

If the first test is: *Does your logo fit in with other industry logos?* Then the second test is: *Does my logo look good next to the logos of companies I would like to sponsor an event with?*

You want to emphatically answer yes to both questions.

Kick Emotional Attachment Out the Door

No matter how much I hit on this next point, there will be somebody who thinks a cartoon teddy bear is a great logo for their coffee shop. They'll argue that the logo has sentimental history behind it—like their young daughter drew it—and isn't it such a perfect representation of the roots of the business and what they're working for?

In short: No. It isn't perfect. Not for people who don't have the associated memory and emotional response you do—which is everyone but you.

I don't mean to sound heartless here…no. Scratch that. I do mean to sound heartless. Because the fact is that if your logo was created by you or anyone you know, you are likely not treating it objectively. This is why I highly recommend having a professional artist design your logo. Once money is on the line, you will become very objective and critical, and that's exactly the mindset you need when designing the face of your business.

A weak design is a weak design. Good intentions don't improve technical execution. And while you may not have the heart to tell that nephew of yours who wants to be an artist when he grows up that he just isn't there yet, chances are you'll fold and use what he gives you to spare his feelings. No one wants to look into the eyes of someone they love and say, "This is subpar and unusable, so how about we just save ourselves a bunch of pain and suffering and admit you're not a fit for this job."

Very few people are willing to have any version of that conversation.

But if a professional sends you a picture of a gopher he designed for a project last year to be a logo for your golf cart company, your response will be swift and strong. You won't try to make the gopher concept work to make the artist feel better. You'll reject the offering and move on.

That's how it should be.

It is not your job to stroke the ego of a budding artist who is still figuring things out. It's your job to create a face that customers can quickly trust and identify. So unless you are an artist who is branding yourself, hire someone to create your logo. Pay someone you have no emotional relationship with to create the final version of your logo. It's the best way to remain objective.

The Exception

There are instances where your actual face will be the face of your company. Actors are an example of this, along with authors, fitness instructors, and others. Making your actual face your logo works just fine so long as you remember that the same rules apply: people remember things in pictures.

This means that you need to become a consistent picture of your brand on and off the clock. Once you brand yourself, people will expect to see consistency. Lack of consistency in even the smallest of acts creates disconnection and distrust as to whether you really are who you say you are.

If you never wear makeup in real life but are all dolled up in your headshot, that's a disconnect. If you're wearing a high-end suit in your profile image but always wear Tommy

Bahama in real life, that's a disconnect. If your brand is upbeat and optimistic and you're having a day where you just can't turn your frown upside-down, that's a disconnect.

Your face can be the face of your business, but if that is your choice you need to keep in mind that people still need brand consistency. Maybe you're consistent in the fact that you never wear the same thing twice, like a celebutante; or maybe you have more of a Steve Jobs turtleneck thing going on. Either way, the important thing is that people know what to expect every time.

For cues on how to best be the face of your brand, look to your style guides. Are there ways you can dress that will help others recognize you in person from across the room? Is there a style that works well on you that you can consistently apply in professional situations? These questions go for men and women both.

You don't need to revamp yourself or transform into something you're not to be the face of your own company, but you may need to assess and edit the visual messages you are sending to others through your visual presentation and voice.

BRAINSTORM TIME

For your logo brainstorming session, I'm going to ask you to do something new: let someone else do the brainstorming for you.

It's finally time to create your logo, and that's not a task for just anyone. Just like you are probably not the right person to design the engine that goes in your car, you are also probably not the right person to create an iconic logo for your brand. And while it's quite possible that you think you already know what your logo looks like, there's a 99% chance that any logo you're imagining at the moment is not your best option.

It's time to let go of preconceived ideas and let a skilled artist take you to higher ground.

The good news is that you've already done all the leg work. If you've completed all the building blocks leading up to this point, then you have everything a strong artist needs to create some strong images for your consideration.

LOGO CONCEPTS I LIKE

Logo

Working With Your Artist

If you've done all the work outlined up to this point, designing your logo will not be a laborious process. In fact, nearly everyone I've ever worked with has had their logos after three rounds of interacting with their artist. If you follow the process below, you should have your logo within a week or two of hiring the artist.

ROUND 1—INITIATION AND CONCEPTS

Start by finding an artist who has created imagery similar to what you would like for your logo. If you can't find an artist you like, use a crowd-sourcing site like 99designs.com to access multiple designers at the same time. Once you've hired them:

1. Introduce yourself and your business by sharing your mission statement with the artist(s)—see Foundation Tier.
2. Tell them the industry you work in—see Personality Tier.
3. Describe the personality of your brand with the artist (e.g., fun-loving, detail-oriented, punctual, luxurious, etc.)—see

Personality Tier.

4. Tell them your brand promise—see Personality Tier.

5. Give them your entire style guide, including font family and color palette—see Style Tier.

6. Give your name and your tagline (both need to incorporate well with the final logo image)—see Style Tier.

7. Show the artist the logos of your competitors (the family your logo should be the most memorable member of) —see Style Tier.

8. Show them the logos of large companies you like—see Style Tier.

9. Share any imagery you think they should consider with people you trust to give valuable feedback.

Once you've done these 9 steps, let your artist work. Set a firm deadline for their first deliverable. In general, three days is usually a good amount of time for your artist to knock some concepts out.

Keep in mind that concept sketches are NOT refined finished products. First round offerings from your artist will be quick mockups to see if you like the approach. Concept image quality will vary from artist to artist, but their job at this point is to see what catches your eye, not deliver diverse perfect images.

ROUND 2—FEEDBACK AND REVISIONS

Once your artist has gotten back to you with your first deliverable, give yourself a few days to develop your feedback, and bring people you trust into the process. More than once I've thought one concept was a clear winner, only to find that everyone else who was less attached my project chose a different design.

Your vote matters, but it will also be biased. So ask around.

Within 72 hours you should get back to your artist and let them know what your top pick(s) is, or if you have directions for a new approach.

Be specific and share the reasons behind your change, if possible (e.g., *"We want to get rid of any points or hard edges in the logo, since our product is known for being soft."* or *"I like option 5, but the landscape layout doesn't work with our packaging. I need a logo with a 1:1 ratio.").* The more your artist understands what you need, the more likely they are to send you something that will blow your mind.

Your feedback should provide the artist with a firm understanding of what you want, because now they're going to start putting some time into any remaining designs so you can see the finished look. Ideally, your artist will only put this level of effort into three designs, or less.

ROUND 3—NAILING IT DOWN

The next round of images you receive should have a finished look to them. This is the point where you approach the designs with a microscope. Give yourself another 72 hours, then reconnect with your artist. If you can sit down with the artist in person and explore changes together, all the better.

By this point in the process there is usually a clear winner. You'll know which one it is because no one will be able to talk you into the other designs. You'll get stubborn, and that's par for the course. Whichever design that is (even if you ditched it back in Round 1), Round 3 is the time and place where you push everything else aside and finish your day with an image you can sign off on.

You're Ready to Go!

Three rounds. That's it. It may seem like that's too fast, but if you've done the work in this book and you have an artist who knows how to make logos, you're going to have a great experience.

Even better, you now have everything you need to get your business up and running. You can now:

- Set up your website
- Make a sign
- Create packaging
- Order business cards, menus, or other printed materials
- Design marketing material
- Put your design on a vehicle

Of course, this is all just the beginning. Now that you've established your brand you need to spend every day living up to it. That requires systems and schedules and training, which are a different matter entirely.

But if you stay true to your branding pyramid your efforts will be focused and consistent, and that will save you a lot of time and money in the long run. So now that you've finished your pyramid, don't put it in a drawer or bury it as a file in a folder on your computer.

Reference your pyramid often. Keep it in a visible place. Share it with people—especially people you hire to work with you. Make it a firm reference point for everyone on your team so that you stay on message and have fewer messes to clean up.

YOUR CUSTOM BRAND PYRAMID

Once your branding pyramid is complete, take a moment to see how simple you've made it for others to understand what you do, how you do it differently, and why they should choose you.

FOUNDATION TIER: THE BEDROCK OF YOUR BUSINESS

Pyramid Element #1: Motto (cornerstone)

Pyramid Element #2: What do you sell?

Pyramid Element #3: Who is your target audience?

Pyramid Element #4: Why should consumers buy your product/service? (What is the difference between you and competitors?)

Pyramid Element #5: What do you stand for?

Pyramid Element #6: How does your company impact the world at large?

Pyramid Element #7: Mission Statement (cornerstone)

PERSONALITY TIER: YOUR HIGH-LEVEL VALUES AND UNIQUE BUSINESS ATTRIBUTES

Pyramid Element #8: Establish your Voice

Pyramid Element #9: Create your Brand Promise

Pyramid Element #10: Define your Values

Pyramid Element #11: Define your Industry and your role within it

Pyramid Element #12: Share your Experience

STYLE TIER: YOUR BRAND'S CONSISTENT VISUAL IDENTITY

Pyramid Element #13: Create the perfect Tagline

Pyramid Element #14: Strategically choose a Name

Pyramid Element #15: Define your Style Guide

THE FACE OF YOUR BRAND: YOUR LOGO

Pyramid Element #16: Your Logo and how to use it

Once you've completed these sixteen elements, you will have a pyramid a six year old can understand and explain to others. And that's exactly what you want: simplicity and clarity when it comes to understanding who you are and what you are about.

CONCLUSION

The more developed your business identity is, the more customers you will attract. Potential customers need to know what you do and why you do it. They should know how you are different, why you're different, and what they're going to get each and every time they interact with you. Experiences create reputation, and that reputation is your brand. It's what people say about you when you're not in the room.

You will know your brand is strong not only when people recognize your brand name and logo on sight, but also when they describe you to others using the exact words you want them to use. You don't need to be as big as Apple or Coca-Cola to make that happen. You just need to be consistent in communicating your four tiers:

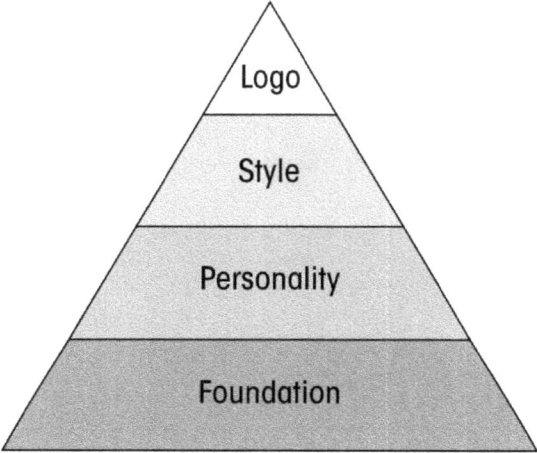

And within those four tiers, always have each of your sixteen building blocks on display in your office or work area, not buried in a file.

Remember to treat each of the sixteen building blocks explored in this book as free employees that work for you 24/7 doing *exactly* what you ask them to do. Approaching each tier of your brand pyramid strategically and consistently will attract your ideal customer. If you're not seeing the results you want to see, chances are that one or more of these pyramid elements needs to be adjusted.

If you're a brand new company, take a stand and give a strong push, but be open to tweaking what needs to be tweaked. And remember that making a branding change is like getting a nose job. You don't get to keep both the old and the new. If you change something, change it. You'll notice that change usually involves an investment of money, but if not changing is losing you money then biting the bullet and moving forward is your power move. Do it.

Ultimately, branding is simple. It is a matter of defining and creating the reputation you want. But the effort required to establish and maintain a brand reputation is what separates the adults from the six year olds.

Living up to a brand is not for sissies. Only

the committed follow through. You can be that brand when you remind yourself that just because something is simple doesn't make it unessential. Because now you know that the opposite is true. It's the little things we do that create consistency, build reputation, and create loyalty.

So go out there and do the little things. Implement the sixteen building blocks of building your brand day-in and day-out, and I guarantee that people will start to take notice of you.

ABOUT THE AUTHOR

Sheralyn's first job was as a karate instructor, which taught her that practice does not make perfect; practice makes habit—good or bad. Martial arts also taught Sheralyn that a master is simply a person who can effortlessly do all the actions a beginner finds difficult or maybe even impossible.

In recent years, Sheralyn has consulted with some of the largest and smallest companies in the world, identifying areas of improvement and designing solutions that help companies grow.

Learn more about Sheralyn and her services by visiting www.WickedSassy.com.

www.WickedSassy.com